Get Things Done

Achieve Monumental Success with Small Actions

By Frederick Weber

Copyright 2015 © All Rights Reserved

Except as permitted as under the U.S. Copyright Act of 1976, no part of this book may be copied, stored, reproduced, republished, uploaded, posted, transmitted, altered or distributed in any way, in whole or part in any form or any medium, or incorporated into any other work, without the express prior written permission except in the case of brief quotations embodied in critical reviews or articles.

Your support of the author's rights is appreciated.

The scanning, uploading and distribution of this book via the Internet or via any other means without the permission of the publisher is illegal and punishable by law. Please purchase only authorized electronic editions, and do not participate in or encourage electronic piracy of copyrighted materials.

Disclaimers:

The information provided within this book is for general informational purposes only. While we try to keep the information up-to-date and correct, there are no representations or warranties, express or implied, about the completeness, accuracy, reliability, suitability or availability with respect to the information, products, services, or related graphics contained in this book for any purpose. Any use of this information is at your own risk.

The author has made every effort to ensure the accuracy of the information within this book was correct at time of publication. The author does not assume and hereby disclaims any liability to any party for any loss, damage, or disruption caused by errors or omissions, whether such errors or omissions result from accident, negligence, or any other cause.

Contents

1: The Power of Setting Small Goals 1
   Goal Setting Basics 2
   Thinking Small Has Big Potential! 4
   Revised Goal Setting Plan 6

2: Goal Setting Mistakes 8

3: Why You Should Break Big Goals Down into Small Actions 12
      Small Goals Keep Your Momentum Going Forward ... 13
      Small Goals Transform Mountains into Hills 13
      Small Goals Develop Belief in Oneself 14
      Small Goals Holds you Accountable 14
      You Will Know What You Want At All Times 15
      We Can Live Life to Its Fullest 16

4: Setting Small Goals Will Help you Overcome Procrastination 17
      What If Goals Don't Have a Deadline? 18
      You Can't Do Everything At Once, So Don't Try! 20

5: Achieving Small Goals Has Huge Psychological Benefits 22
      Small Goals Give you Hope 22
      Take Control 23
      Gain Experience While you Succeed 23
      Small Goals Makes it Easier to Focus on your Strengths 24

6: Achieve Huge Success by Thinking Small 25
      Ready to Get Started? 25
      Create a Visual Plan of Action 26
      Group Tasks and Set a Deadline 27
      Deciding How Much Time a Goal Requires 28
      What Will You Need to Achieve the Small Goal? 28
      Always Focus on the Goal you are On Rather than your End Goal 29

Final Thoughts 30

1

The Power of Setting Small Goals

In an ideal world, we would be halfway through our list of goals at the halfway point of any given year. Sometimes that can be the case but there are many who constantly struggle to achieve their goals. Reaching that halfway point of the year only serves as an unpleasant reminder that those goals are falling further behind schedule. Does this sound like something that you're dealing with? If the answer to that question is yes, then you have found the perfect book. Sit back and take a good long look at your situation. What's standing in your way?

Are your goals just too big to accomplish?

Are you just unlucky?

Are you not motivated enough to give yourself that extra push?

While some of these might be true, it all boils down to one fact. You have been told to "think big" throughout your entire life. While that's good advice, sometimes the thing that's blocking you from achieving your larger goals is the fact that you're not thinking small enough. That might be contrary to everything you've been taught growing up but thinking small is just as important of a process as thinking big. The two powers go hand-in-hand.

Let's start off by taking a look at the goal setting process that most people use. There's no shortage of books and videos that teach these goal setting techniques.

Goal Setting Basics

All goal setting techniques generally follow the same pattern and that pattern looks something like this:

1. Envision what it is that you want.

2. Create accountability by telling your friends and family.

3. Set a deadline.

4. Break it down into smaller, manageable steps.

5. Network with professionals who have accomplished similar goals and then model their systems.

6. Believe in your goal.

7. Take big action.

8. Repeat steps 6 and 7.

The problem is not that these steps don't work. On the contrary, they work just fine. The real problem lies with step 6. Often times, we set such huge goals that it's difficult to truly believe that they are even possible. Sure, we can tell ourselves that it's possible until we're blue in the face but actually believing it is a different story. That belief is just as important as taking action since it's your belief in being successful that motivates you to take action. Think of belief as a muscle that you have to exercise. If you do nothing, then it remains weak and is essentially useless.

By setting large goals, we are unintentionally requiring our belief to be just as large in order to support it. Many people fall into the trap of mistaking desire for belief. There is a huge difference between wanting a thing and believing it.

Here's what happens when you set a big goal but only have a small belief that it's possible:

1. We set this huge goal that is aligned with something that we've promised ourselves for a long period of time.

2. We then try to motivate ourselves by really wanting it. We tell ourselves something like, "If I really want to achieve it, then I have to really want it!"

3. We lay out a plan of action.

4. We follow that plan for several weeks.

5. Oops! We miss a deadline and then suddenly start spiraling off course. That one missed deadline turns into another and then we fail hard!

Something always seems to come up that stops us from achieving that goal. Last minute plans come up and we allow ourselves to be spurred into those plans. A computer crashes and we find ourselves dealing with this issue instead of keeping up with the weekly to-do list.

All of that stuff leads to guilt and eventually our defensive reaction kicks in. That defensive reaction to failure is procrastination. "I'll restart this step on Monday." I will admit that I've fallen prey to this reaction on several occasions. It's not fun. When things get sour then it's difficult to keep pushing forward. Procrastination is the number one destroyer of passion and motivation! The problem is that it sneaks up on us so quickly that we don't even notice its happening. "I'll restart this step on Monday" seems like a logical course of action at the time, but in reality it's just a form of procrastination that destroys dreams.

This kind of thinking can turn a passionate individual into a disheartened goal setter who falls into the trap of setting goals day-after-day, year-after-year but never really gets anywhere. A good example of this is a person who sets New Year's Resolutions every year, yet gives up in a month or two and then waits until the following year to try again. The result is just disappointment.

What's the solution to this reoccurring problem?

The answer is simple – start thinking small.

Thinking Small Has Big Potential!

This book is going to show you how thinking small can offer real solutions to big problems. We just went through the basics of how goal setting works by demonstrating a more traditional method. However, those traditional methods are all limited by the belief that the individual truly possesses. I feel compelled to point out that you cannot manufacture belief – you either have it or you don't. You cannot simply look in a mirror and say "I believe" 100 times, expecting it to magically happen. It won't!

With all of this in mind, let's look at some super small goals. Our goal with this book is to create incremental goals that are going to develop your belief in a larger goal. So we are talking about taking super small steps here. Let me give you a couple of examples.

If your big goal is to start your own business, then you would start with something like **"read one business book this week"** or **"interview one business owner this week."**

If your goal is to lose 30 pounds, then you would start with something like **"eat one healthy meal this week"**, **"remove one food from my diet"**, or **"exercise for 15 minutes one time this week."**

You are essentially turning your large goal into a super small one. This helps you build momentum. Nothing under the sun builds momentum faster than getting a few successes under your belt! Just don't forget that you still want to dream big but you will need to build momentum towards those big goals. Accomplishing a goal is much more fulfilling than taking a step towards a goal. It might sound like the same thing but it's really a much different process. A step towards a goal gets you closer to achieving it but accomplishing a small goal in itself will develop your belief. This belief will empower you so that you can accomplish those big goals that might seem impossible now.

Now let's look at a revised version of the same goal setting template that we listed earlier.

Revised Goal Setting Plan

Your revised plan will look something like this:

1. Look back at all of those huge goals that you have set in the past but failed to accomplish. Keep this list for future reference.

2. Now choose the goal that you would like to accomplish the most. Write it down.

3. Transform that goal into a smaller goal that you could accomplish in one week's time.

4. Complete that small goal.

5. Repeat Steps 3 and 4 with that same large goal but make each goal just a little bit larger each time. Do this until you have accomplished about 5 goals.

6. Once you have about 5 goals under your belt, you can then tackle that larger goal.

I'm not saying that all of your large goals can be solved with just five small goals. Some will require a lot more smaller goals before you can build the momentum to achieve them. The point here is that it's a whole lot easier to move up a large hill once you have built momentum than it is to start from a stand-still. The same is true of accomplishing large goals.

Just like with belief, motivation is something that you cannot purchase or manufacture, no matter how much you might want to. Momentum is earned through success. Once you get moving, keep going.

No one sets out to start a seven-figure business during the first week. Those who are successful start out with small goals in mind. For example, we might start with a goal of earning enough money to pay our internet bill every month, then move up to earning enough to pay our rent, and eventually we can start earning enough to pay all of our bills. While the big goal is always to earn seven-figures, it is not a viable goal to have early on.

Whatever big dreams you might have, I encourage you to put them to the side for now and focus on smaller goals. Build some momentum and earn belief in that long-term goal.

2

Goal Setting Mistakes

Before we get started, I feel that it's important to go through some of the most common mistakes that people make when setting goals. Avoiding these mistakes will give you a huge advantage. I tend to see these same things repeated by numerous people. So, the first step to learning to set small goals is to learn from these mistakes. Let's get started.

Mistake #1: Not Writing it Down

So many people tell themselves, "Oh I can remember that so why do I need to write it down?" Let me ask a counter question: why wouldn't you write it down? I'm sorry but anyone who is too lazy to take the time to write down their goals is not going to get very far in achieving them.

Writing down goals makes you accountable, frees up your mind, and essentially transforms an aspiration into reality. Unless it's written down on paper, it is nothing more than a lifeless aspiration. It has absolutely no meaning. By committing to write it down, you are breathing life into the goal. Only then can you truly focus on attaining that goal.

Mistake #2: Creating Too Many Goals at Once

Over time you're going to create and achieve hundreds of goals. There will even be times when you might have to chase after two goals at the same time. One instance would be if your goal requires money that you don't have at that moment. Then you would have a second goal where you raise that money. This book is going to focus on creating small goals so that, in most cases, you will only be working towards no more than two goals at any one moment.

Mistake #3: Only Setting Goals in One Area of Life

Most people put all of their focus on setting career goals so they completely forget about setting personal goals. Life goes above and beyond just your career. If you want to live the richest life possible, then you should be setting both professional and personal goals. Use the same strategies in this book to make the most of both areas.

Mistake #4: Not Setting Specific Goals

This is probably the most common goal setting mistake. Most people set extremely vague goals. Some examples of vague goals include "I want to start a business" or "I want to lose weight." These are just not specific enough. For a goal to be worthwhile, it needs to define a specific course of action. That brings us to our next mistake.

Mistake #5: Not Creating Measurable Goals

This goes hand-in-hand with creating goals that are too vague. Goals have to be quantified so that you can track them. For example, saying that "I want to start a real estate business" or "I want to lose 30 pounds" are quantifiable. Of course, this book is going to show you how to break these down into smaller goals but I just want you to understand that one of the most important aspects of goal setting is being able to measure it.

Mistake #6: Failure to Set Deadlines

Deadlines create a sense of urgency. They force us to pay attention to what is important. If you do not set deadlines then there is not going to be any urgency pushing you complete those goals. That makes it tempting to procrastinate. We will actually discuss this in greater detail later in this book.

Mistake #7: Not Displaying Goals

Writing down goals is important but having them displayed where you have to see them on a daily basis makes them even more powerful. Small goals that you will be setting by using the strategies in this book are only going to take a week or two to complete, so it's even more important that you make them visible.

Mistake #8: Living in a Comfort Zone

Safe goals are not going to fulfill your lifelong ambitions. Until you leave your comfort zone, you're not going to create any real success. While goals certainly should always be achievable, they should also push you to the limits. By using the strategies in this book, you will be transforming intimidating goals that might scare you into manageable, realistic, small goals that can deliver life-changing results.

Mistake #9: Setting Boring Goals

Goals that do not personally compel you to pursue something meaningful for your life are useless. The purpose of a goal is to accomplish something that betters your life. However, most people get stuck somewhere in between. So be sure that you are setting goals that are pushing you to better yourself.

Mistake #10: Failing to Break Large Goals Down into Small Goals

Setting big goals is only the first step but if you ever hope to achieve them then you're going to need to break them down into small goals. These small goals hold a lot of power. They keep you motivated to push forward, even when things get tough. However, I feel that their greatest benefit is the momentum that they generate. It's this momentum that will propel you forward. If you focus on a large goal, then you are going to spend all of your days being intimidated. That intimidation leads to procrastination, which will eventually lead to huge failures.

This book is going to show you how to unlock this power for yourself.

3

Why You Should Break Big Goals Down into Small Actions

I'm sure that you've read several articles or listened to multiple seminars about the power of setting goals but many of these tend to miss one pivotal point that might be the most important part of the process. We all know the importance of setting goals but what's even more important is to set the right goals.

If you were planning a trip from New York to California, you wouldn't just say, "Okay, I'm driving west until I eventually hit California!"

At least, I hope you wouldn't do that! Instead, you would use a map or a map application to plan the route. That plan would be laid out into several steps that include steps like this:

1. Go onto I-80 W

2. Merge onto I-80 W via the exit on the left toward Des Moines

3. Merge onto I-76 W via exit 102 on the left toward Denver

These are small incremental goals that allow you to stay on track without getting lost. That same philosophy is used to plan out large goals. Planning small goals has a ton of benefits.

Small Goals Keep Your Momentum Going Forward

Having a manageable goal written down staring you in the face gives you something to work towards. You can wake up and get started right away, instead of just winging it. Smaller goals serve as constant reminders of what you need to accomplish on a short-term basis. It's easy to get lost with long-term goals when something goes wrong but smaller goals are much easier to keep up with during the most difficult times.

There is one common pattern that develops when working towards a goal that's easy to envision. It excites you to work even harder, which makes it easy to stay motivated. Since smaller goals are much easier to visualize, then that motivation is always at its peak. We lose motivation when we lose our vision. As you successfully achieve these small goals, you will build momentum that will allow you to set even bigger goals. That brings us to the next advantage of setting smaller goals.

Small Goals Transform Mountains into Hills

Big goals often seem impossible to achieve since their end is so far in the future. It's easy to lose momentum while trying to climb such a huge mountain. Using our traveling example from above, it's hard to see your destination when you are still at the beginning of your journey. Sure, envisioning a long-term goal is great but it's simply not possible to climb such a steep mountain without building some momentum first.

Setting small goals transforms these large aspirations into achievable stepping stones. Then you are working towards a goal that you know is achievable. Belief in your end goal becomes stronger as you achieve each smaller goal.

Small Goals Develop Belief in Oneself

Remember, belief is a muscle that must be developed by achieving success. When starting out with a new goal, your belief in that goal will be at its weakest. Therefore, you need to develop that belief by achieving small measures of success. Setting goals is not simply a matter of holding yourself accountable; it's about fueling that belief.

Do you want to keep on dreaming or do you want to actually accomplish something worthwhile? Everyone dreams but only a handful of people actually turn those dreams into reality. Unless you take action, you will never achieve that long-term goal. How could you? When you see yourself making slow progress, it fuels your belief a little more each day until you finally come to a point where you can no longer see yourself failing.

Small Goals Holds you Accountable

If you ever want to achieve anything worthwhile, then you can go ahead and count on failing multiple times. That's not being pessimistic; that's just the way it is. When you are trying to achieve a huge goal and you fail, then it's almost impossible to see the details of where and how that failure happened. When you are working with small goals, it's easy to see those details. So smaller goals make it much easier to re-evaluate and plan your next path when you fail.

By setting small goals, you have the powerful ability to make changes in real time. If you are simply working off of a long-term goal then it could be a year later before you realize that you're nowhere even close to achieving your goal. Then you are left wondering why instead of being able to take action to fix it.

You Will Know What You Want At All Times

Sometimes we tend to set goals that don't really reflect our truest desires. What I mean is that we might believe that we want more money but we actually just need to change our environment. Other times we might believe that we want more time but what we really want is to find work that we truly enjoy.

If you do not set goals, then there is no way of knowing what you truly want. So what happens if we set a huge goal that is not reflective of our true desire? We are stuck with this huge goal that we're hesitant to change. However, when you are working with smaller goals, it's much easier to change the next step to match your truest desire. You can even re-evaluate that goal altogether!

Re-assessing our goals is a powerful tool that will reap huge rewards. It helps to figure out what it is that we truly want. By setting small goals, you are able to adjust them to match your desires as you reflect on yourself.

We Can Live Life to Its Fullest

It's much more fulfilling to live life working towards achieving goals than it is to just wing it. Most of the best experiences are not going to be handed to you on a silver platter. You have to earn them. By setting small goals, you are setting yourself up for success. There is no greater feeling in this world than to be successful.

Now, I'm not saying that you should go out and plan every single moment of your entire life. After all, what fun is life without a little adventure here and there? Setting goals allows you to live your personal life without the constant worry of never fulfilling your goals. Setting small goals allows you to be successful very quickly. You will know that your life is going in the right direction, so you can enjoy it more.

4

Setting Small Goals Will Help you Overcome Procrastination

Overcoming procrastination is one of the most essential components to achieving success. The tendency to put things off is a huge hurdle that must be overcome. What makes it even worse is that in most cases, we don't even realize that we're procrastinating. We tell ourselves things like:

"I will restart this on Monday so that I have a fresh start."

Or

"I can start this tomorrow when I have more time."

The truth is that without having small goals in place, you simply have no way of knowing when you are procrastinating. Avoiding procrastination starts with setting goals. Simply getting started is one of the best ways to avoid procrastinating. Now I ask you this: is it easier to get started when you can see the finish line or when the finish line is out of sight? Naturally, if the journey seems short, then it's going to be much easier to get started right away. People tend to put off huge goals to begin at the beginning of the day, week, month, quarter, or even year. However, when you are working to achieve smaller goals, then you will be compelled to start immediately. Think about how many people wait until the start of the New Year to start trying to achieve their goal of losing 50 pounds. What if you changed that goal to losing 2 pounds? Wouldn't that motivate you to start right away? Set small goals and you will be better motivated to start sooner rather than later.

Now let's expand on that just a bit further. If you set small goals, then your deadlines are going to seem more urgent. Have you ever crammed for an exam? Looming deadlines have powerful effects on our productivity. When you are dealing with a long-term goal, the deadline is so far away that urgency is not a factor. However, when you are dealing with small goals, then you will have deadlines that are within sight. Therefore, urgency once again plays a powerful role.

What If Goals Don't Have a Deadline?

There will be times that goals in your life might be ongoing, so those particular goals might not have deadlines. One example would be a goal of losing weight. If you weigh 180 lbs. and you want to lose 50 lbs., then once you achieve that goal, your ongoing goal would be to maintain a weight of 130 lbs.

If you have an ongoing goal, then you will need to set a specific goal each week so that you are clear as to what you need to do in order to maintain that ongoing goal.

You always want to set deadlines when possible but you need to consider your schedule as you set goals. Another huge factor in procrastination is over-commitment. Sometimes we give ourselves too many tasks to accomplish. Then we are forced to put things off. Plus, it tends to drain the life right out of you!

Now we come to one of the biggest procrastination scenarios and that is when a goal seems so big that you simply have no idea where to start. That's why setting small goals is so powerful; it makes starting a whole lot less intimidating. Plus, the starting point itself is even clearer. When you successfully complete one goal, then you can set another and your momentum will propel you right into that next goal. Every time you complete a goal it becomes a lot easier to get started with the next.

That brings us to setting a goal that ends up involving more than you expected. Sometimes when you are venturing into new areas, you will discover that your initial plan is just not going to cut it. Maybe there's an additional cost or the process takes much longer than you had expected? Whatever the case, most individuals will simply put that task to the side and restart it at a later date. If you are dealing with large goals, then these issues become much more difficult to manage. It becomes so stressful that we put off the task until we have had time to rethink the overall approach. Sometimes this can take several weeks.

On the other hand, running into these types of issues with small goals is easily manageable. You will be able to determine exactly what is needed and not lose your momentum. Lessening your expectations will give you more insight into the exact details of what you need to get done.

You Can't Do Everything At Once, So Don't Try!

This is a realization that hits all of us in the face like a splash of cold water. At first, it's an unpleasant feeling but it eventually becomes refreshing. I want you to understand right now that you cannot do everything. Your time is limited and once spent, you never get it back. Time management impacts you in huge ways. So many individuals fall into the trap of having so many tasks on their to-do list that they wind up swapping back and forth so much that their productivity suffers.

Traditional goal setting tells us that we have to prioritize our commitments. That's great advice but this is where small goals really become a blessing. It's much easier to prioritize your daily tasks when you are dealing with small goals because they give you so much clarity. All you really have to do is prioritize those tasks using the following categories:

Importance: More important tasks should always be listed first.

Enjoyment: Mixing in tasks that are enjoyable keeps your daily routine from becoming too tedious.

Again, managing small goals is a lot easier than dealing with monumental goals. There are several crossroads with all big goals that come up. We have to choose which task to complete first. With small goals, these crossroads are usually negated because we are simplifying the process.

Procrastination can sometimes be the result of a lack of information or skills. In these cases, it's much easier to just put off the task instead of researching and learning new skills. Setting smaller goals makes it less intimidating to learn these skills since they can be taken on in small chunks.

5

Achieving Small Goals Has Huge Psychological Benefits

Having a focus in your life gives you direction; it brings order to chaos. Of course, having goals that are too large create their own form of chaos, while smaller goals tend to narrow your focus. Before we continue, I want to go through some of the psychological benefits that come from setting small goals.

Small Goals Give you Hope

You always have something to look forward to. When you are dealing with small goals, you will be able to see results on a weekly or bi-weekly basis in most cases. Therefore, you're going to be filled with a newfound sense of hope every time you complete one of these small goals. Consider how much easier it is to wake up early in the morning when you have an exciting day ahead of you.

It works both ways though. If your goals are too big, then you're going to have a tough time seeing the finish line. That makes it easy to lose hope and decreases your optimism. Some people have enough vision to work through these large goals but for most of us, we need to achieve success at regular intervals in order to feel as if we are moving forward.

Take Control

Achieving small goals quickly adds up into a lot of tiny victories. Who needs New Year's Resolutions when we can set goals every day of the year? Take control of your own dreams by giving yourself a psychological boost. There is no greater feeling than to be in control of your own life.

Once you succeed at achieving just a couple of small goals, then you're going to feel a major shift in your attitude. "Maybe" transforms into "definitely." Confidence plays a major role in achieving long-term success.

Gain Experience While you Succeed

Here's one of the greatest psychological benefits of setting smaller goals that lead up to your overall, large goal. You will gain valuable experience as you work your way closer to your goal. Furthermore, you will gain that experience without the high risk associated with taking on large goals. Let me explain.

Failure is often our greatest teacher. It teaches us our most valuable lessons. When you are dealing with small goals, then those failures will be much smaller. Now here's the best part. They will teach you the same lessons without doing nearly as much damage. You can simply refocus your goal and begin anew; whereas if you are focusing on a large goal, you would have to consume a lot of energy re-planning.

Small Goals Makes it Easier to Focus on your Strengths

Basic goal setting teaches us that we should try to focus on our strengths but sometimes that's easier said than done. Large goals are so broad that they require so many constant tweaks that it's hard to pay attention to focusing on strengths. However, when you set smaller goals, then you are in more control.

The whole point of trying to achieve your long-term goals is to enjoy a more fulfilling life. Make it as easy on yourself as you possibly can.

6

Achieve Huge Success by Thinking Small

Having a goal to aim for is a powerful tool but if you have to spend too much time working towards the same goal, then it suddenly becomes intimidating and demoralizing. By now, I'm sure that you understand that we keep this from happening by creating small goals as stepping stones to our large ones. What we have not really gotten into is how that's accomplished.

Whether you're looking to make a change in your life or business, this is the process that you will use in order to break down that large intimidating goal into small, manageable goals.

By setting small, achievable goals along the way, you are going to develop your belief in the overall goal. That belief will keep you motivated at every step.

Ready to Get Started?

The initial layout is what takes the most time. You want to start with your end goal in mind and then work backwards. Consider the basics of what you need to happen in order for you to achieve your long-term goal.

For example, if you are starting a business, then your goal would be to make a profit. Therefore, you will need a few great products and/or services in order to achieve that goal. If you work further backwards, you will then start to see much smaller steps. Just keep brainstorming backwards, writing everything down.

By the time you are finished, you should have listed a lot of stuff. You want every step that you list to be achievable within no more than a couple of weeks.

Create a Visual Plan of Action

Now that you have all of this stuff written down, get a blank sheet of paper and list your large goal at the top of the page. Now find a specific area and work backwards, listing each smaller goal below. Do so until you are all the way at the beginning. All of these "steps" will actually be a small goal. Let's use our example from above to show you what it will look like.

12. Generate Six Figure Profits from my New Business

11. Set up AdWords Marketing

10. Set up Facebook Ads

9. Start a Blog

8. Build a Website

7. Create a LinkedIn Profile

6. Create a Facebook Page

5. Create a Facebook Profile

4. Create the Product/Service

3. Research Competition

2. Research Niche

1. Find Niche

Keep in mind that this is just a general idea that I am using as an example. You would probably add several steps to this process but this is enough to give you an idea. Also note that the list is numbered from bottom to top. The bottom task would come first. You can even group certain tasks together if needed.

Wouldn't it be much easier to start off by just finding a niche versus starting with the daunting task of generating six figure profits?

Group Tasks and Set a Deadline

While most people might teach you to lay out a timetable for the entire list now, I recommend that you only set a deadline for your first small goal. Using the same example from above, I would start off with something like this:

<u>Small Goal 1</u>

1. Find Niche

2. Research Niche

3. Research Competition

Deadline: 1 Week

By starting with a small goal like this, you are able to focus your attention on just research. You don't have to worry about trying to earn a profit at this point. You are simply trying to find a niche for your first product/service. Since you know that doing just this one task will lead you closer to your ultimate goal, you will not feel the stress of your large goal. Plus, I believe that you will find a much better niche if you spend this much time on it than you would if you rushed it.

Deciding How Much Time a Goal Requires

This part can be a little tricky. If you choose a timeframe that is too far away, then you might procrastinate because you won't feel the urgency from the looming deadline. However, if you don't give yourself enough time to realistically achieve your goal, then you are setting yourself up for mistakes. One week for the above example is a perfect deadline. If you finish early, then you can always start on the next step.

What Will You Need to Achieve the Small Goal?

Finally, our last (and probably most important) step to planning out a small goal is to determine what you will need to make it happen. Consider any tools, knowledge, skills, assistance, or costs that you will need in order to achieve the goal.

There will be times when you might need to create a separate goal in order to get the resources required to complete it. For example, if your goal is to set up an advertising campaign, then you might have to set a small goal for getting the money to fund it.

Always Focus on the Goal you are On Rather than your End Goal

Setting these small goals does absolutely no good if you continuously focus on your end goal. Try and keep your attention on achieving the small goal at hand and then move to the next. Imagine if you were standing at the foot of a massive mountain that reached high into the clouds. If you were planning to climb that mountain, would it be easier to focus on reaching the top or to just focus on reaching the first campsite that is only a hundred feet above where you are currently standing?

Working with small goals will make your life much easier but only if you put all of your focus on each small goal. Don't allow yourself to be tempted to gaze at the large goal. It will only intimidate you. Instead, enjoy each small triumph as you work your way up.

Final Thoughts

By now, you have learned the importance of breaking down your larger goals into small, manageable steps. While having this knowledge is a great benefit, it will do you no good unless you actually take action. Remember that the first step to success is knowledge. You have that now but you have to take the next step by putting that knowledge to practical use. Here is a quick recap on the most important tips to keep in mind as you continue on your journey to creating a successful life.

Don't be afraid to dream big but remember to plan small.

Avoid the critical mistakes that many people make when setting goals – the biggest of which is that they create unmanageable goals that are impossible to accomplish.

Never put off tasks. Start on them as soon as possible. There is absolutely no difference in starting a new goal on Thursday afternoon and starting it on Monday morning; so why wait?

Set deadlines to create a sense of urgency. Urgency plays a powerful role in motivating us to keep pushing forward.

If you don't write it down, it is only a lifeless ambition. Write down your goals and what you will need in order to achieve them.

Always keep your full attention on goals you need to accomplish now rather than daydreaming about achieving your long-term goal.

www.ingramcontent.com/pod-product-compliance
Lightning Source LLC
Chambersburg PA
CBHW020958180526
45163CB00006B/2414